Perspectives
Putting Animals to Work
What Are the Issues?

Series Consultant: Linda Hoyt

Flying Start to Literacy®

Contents

What are the limits to how we should use and control animals?

People and animals have shared the earth for a very long time. About 10 to 15 thousand years ago, humans began domesticating and controlling animals. They trained animals such as dogs and horses to help them work. And they bred and raised other animals for food.

Animals still work for us today. They entertain us. They take our place when new drugs are tested.

What are our obligations to the animals that work for us?

Training elephants

Based on scientific research and his practical experience of training, Dr Andrew McLean created a program called HELP (Human Elephant Learning Programs) for the humane training of elephants. With the support of the Wildlife Trust of India, he has conducted regional workshops in India. He is now working in other parts of Asia.

Some people believe that elephants should not be trained to work for us. What would you say to these people?

Dr Andrew McLean

Should we take wild animals and train them to work for us? Wouldn't they be better off in the wild?

I work with people in India who train elephants to work, and I have been asked this question frequently.

Although many people believe that it would be nice if all elephants could be allowed to roam freely, the reality is that this is rarely possible. As the elephants' natural habitat rapidly dwindles so too does the number of wild elephants. Therefore, it is possible that in the future, Asian wild elephants will exist mostly on managed ranges, in national parks and in zoos. If elephants are trained humanely, and the amount of work they do is heavily regulated, then I see no need to ban their limited use, especially if they can help save themselves and other endangered species.

Why do people train elephants?

The communities we work in are ones where elephants have been a vital part of agriculture and forestry for many centuries. These communities rely on elephants and they play a very important role in their economy, their history and their culture.

The elephants we train are used in agriculture and forestry. They are used in national parks to find and deter poachers, and to protect wild populations of endangered species. They are helping to stamp out poaching, which is rapidly decimating elephants, tigers and rhinos across Asia. Well-trained elephants provide the best "vehicle" for stealthily capturing poachers.

What is the traditional method of training elephants?

In South East Asia, elephant training first began around 6000 years ago. Unfortunately, it traditionally involves techniques that cause physical damage to the animals. The idea is to make each elephant submit to the commands of their mahout *– the person who trains, rides and looks after the elephant.*

The elephants are tied up and dragged into a rough wooden crate known as a training crush. They are isolated, hungry and frightened. During their training, they get hit with sticks fitted with rusty nails. They don't have any water or food for up to a week. When they are working, they get beaten for every mistake they make. These painful experiences make the elephants anxious and potentially dangerous.

Dr Andrew McLean meets with elephant trainers.

What is your method of training elephants?

Elephant training, like the training of all animals, is only cruel when it is done badly or with the wrong motives. When elephants are trained gently and have reliable habits, training does not threaten their welfare.

The biggest difference between my method and traditional ones is that we don't inflict pain or punish the elephants to make them submissive. We try to get the elephants to respond to predictable commands and reliable cues such as voice commands, applying pressure, food rewards and touch instead of inflicting pain or punishing them. I want to make the training ethical and safer for both the elephants and the mahouts.

What are the benefits of your training methods?

Elephants learn faster, work with more skill and become safer for people to work with, when compared to elephants that have received the commonly used pain-based training. Elephants can take less than ten days to reach the same level of learning that once took two to three months.

Safety is improved because the elephant stays calm and focused. This prevents injuries that can happen to the mahouts *when an elephant that has experienced pain-based training suddenly panics. Many* mahouts *are killed each year because of this.*

The long-term improvement in safety is mainly due to better everyday handling. Also, the mahouts *feel better about the way they train their animals because they do not necessarily want to hurt the elephants. They were training them in the only way that they knew.*

Dr Andrew McLean formed the not-for-profit group HELP Foundation (Human Elephant Learning Programs), bringing together a team of experts. You can find out more at: h-elp.org

Battery hens should be banned

Today, most people living in cities buy their eggs from the supermarket and, when they do, they often have a choice – free-range or battery-hen eggs.

Here, 12-year-old Tess Quinn tells us why we should choose free-range eggs.

Are you persuaded by her argument? How does she try to persuade you?

Firstly, what are battery hens? The term "battery hens" comes from the industrial approach to housing and farming hens. The hens are put in wire cages side-by-side. The cages are like the cells of batteries – that's how battery hens got their name.

To begin with, the hens are kept in extremely poor conditions. Their cages are very small. Each hen has about 170 to 195 square centimetres of space. The whole cage is completely made out of wire. Frequently, hens lose feathers when they rub against the metal bars. It's also very unhealthy for their feet to always be clutching onto the metal. The poor conditions stop them from living life as a chicken should. They can't carry on with their natural behaviours such as taking dirt baths, stretching, exercising, foraging and socialising.

When the hens are put into the cages, they are under a lot of stress, which causes them to be aggressive. The hens tend to gang up on their fellow cage mates and peck at each other.

The point of battery farms is for farmers to cheaply and easily make money. There are 18 million egg-laying hens in Australia and 70 per cent of these hens are kept in cages! But think about it, if the chickens aren't healthy, does that make your eggs healthy? So don't just pick the cheaper option, choose the option that's healthier for you and saves chickens.

No animal deserves to be treated like these hens are. So, if you believe in making a difference and stopping this abuse, then be a voice for them. Spread the word to help save these poor, innocent animals. Buy only free-range eggs. Hens that are free-range are given more space and better living conditions.

Fresh free-range eggs

Lights! Camera! Bark!

Ever wondered how they get dogs to perform daring rescue scenes or bark on cue in your favourite movies and television shows? Lots of hard work goes on behind the scenes to make sure the animals are not mistreated or exploited. Here, Kathiann M. Kowalski explains how.

Do you think these performing animals really have a happy life? How are their lives different? What are they missing out on?

From rescue dogs to rescue scenes

"We're looking for animals that are outgoing and people-friendly," says trainer Mathilde de Cagny at Birds & Animals Unlimited in California in the United States. She has trained dozens of star canines.

"About 80 per cent of the dogs and cats that are used in film are shelter rescues or shelter placements," notes Marie Belew Wheatley, president and CEO of the American Humane Association (AHA). "These are animals that have been saved and go on to be actors." Even if prior owners had trouble handling them, trainers can work with most problem behaviours except biting.

Many animals used in movies come from animal shelters. Animals who take directions well are trained for movies; new owners adopt those that don't.

Ready on the set!

"It takes about four months, if you spend every day, to get a good trained dog," says de Cagny. Acting dogs learn lots of behaviours to look like they belong in a story. They also learn to behave professionally so that they don't disrupt others on the set.

On screen, it may look like the dog comes when an actor calls his character's name. In reality, the trainer is about five metres away, standing behind the camera and using hand gestures or other signals to cue the dog.

Many different dogs are used to play the one dog character in most movies.

Do animals do their own stunts?

If a dog whimpers on screen, the animal seems hurt or sad. But that's all right if the trainer taught the behaviour and the animal wasn't really hurt, either physically or psychologically. Likewise, computer-assisted technology can make it look as though an animal went flying through the air when it didn't. What counts is how productions treat acting animals in real life.

To reassure viewers, many film productions invite safety representatives of the American Humane Association (AHA) to visit their sets. Following detailed guidelines, representatives check to make sure that animals have adequate food and water. Are they comfortable – not too hot or too cold? Representatives also make sure that no cruelty is used to get the response seen on screen.

If the production passes muster, the AHA awards an end credit, stating that no animals were harmed in the making of the film. "By and large, producers want to do the right thing," notes Wheatley. "After all, viewers care that acting animals receive humane treatment. That means a happy ending for everyone."

Apes need rights

As we learn more about the culture and emotions of the great apes, a controversy is heating up over whether they should have "person" status under the law. Here, Pamela S. Turner, Peg Lopata and Kathiann M. Kowalski look at both sides of the issue as it pertains to apes used in medical research.

Do you think it is right to use apes for medical research? Read the argument against (point) and the argument for (counterpoint). Then you can decide.

Point:

Apes need rights

About 1100 chimpanzees are being used in biomedical research in the United States right now. Jane Goodall, author of *Reason for Hope,* has worked for many decades to improve conditions for research animals, but she would like to see the practice come to an end.

In her book she writes: "What is done to animals in the name of science is often, from the animals' point of view, pure torture – and would be regarded as such if perpetrated by anyone who was not a scientist."

In 1999, all of the European Union nations signed the Treaty of Amsterdam, which recognises these animals as capable of feeling fear and pain. Since 1999, countries such as New Zealand, Great Britain, the Netherlands, Sweden and Austria have banned medical research that uses chimpanzees. The only two countries besides the United States that still allow biomedical research on chimps are China and Japan.

"The United States is sorrowfully, pitifully behind," says Professor Marc Beckoff from the University of Colorado–Boulder in the United States. "It's a very sad situation when we have to grant chimpanzees legal rights in order to protect them. Why don't we just do that out of the goodness of our hearts?" To save human lives is no excuse for hurting or killing animals, Beckoff insists.

Goodall responds to such thinking in her book *Reason for Hope*. She states that even if the animals are bred for the purpose of medical research, "Does this make them somehow less pig? Less monkey? Less dog? Does this deprive them of feelings and the capacity to suffer? If we raised humans for medical experiments, would they be less human and suffer less and matter less than other humans?"

Jane Goodall has committed much of her life to studying chimpanzees in the wild.

People dressed as gorillas take part in a charity event to raise money for gorilla conservation.

Some animal rights advocates want person status for all animals with developed emotions and intellects. “Chimpanzees, bonobos, gorillas and orangutans experience emotions in much the same way as humans do,” says Sarah Baeckler from the Animal Legal Defense Fund. “They express happiness, sadness, fear, sorrow and all sorts of other emotions.”

They also appear to be capable of empathy, altruism, self-awareness and cooperation. Dr Frans de Waal, from Emory University in Atlanta, in the United States, says that the fact that chimpanzees groom each other shows they have a sense of fairness and sharing.

Chimps have also been observed helping a frightened young chimp down from a tree, an example of empathy. Dr de Waal has noted that female chimpanzees have removed stones from the hands of males about to fight. Other scientists have observed a group of chimpanzees consoling the loser in a fight between two chimps.

Steven Wise, an animal rights lawyer, concludes, “We shouldn’t do anything to a great ape that you wouldn’t do to a human. Whether we need to do it or not, it’s wrong.”

Counterpoint:

Research on apes helps cure human disease

"Animal research has been responsible for nearly every medical health advancement we have today," says Jim Newman of the Oregon Health and Science University, in Portland, in the United States. He points out that advancements in medical care for animals depend upon using animals in research, too. Vaccines such as polio, tetanus, diphtheria, Hepatitis B and smallpox were all developed by being tested on animals.

There are rules that control animal research. But, according to Tom Gordon, also from Emory University, in Atlanta, in the United States, "the ethical guideline under which we work is: You don't work with live animals when there's an alternative approach available that would allow you to gain the same information."

Retired laboratory chimps, which have been used in biomedical research, hang out in their enclosure at the National Chimpanzee Sanctuary in Louisiana, USA.

According to the researchers, nobody wants to use animals unless it is completely necessary. "The only way to answer some complex questions, especially those regarding understanding disease, is by using a whole, living organism," says Dr Eric Sandgren, from the University of Wisconsin–Madison in the United States.

Thanks to animal advocates and concerned researchers, animal care practices continue to improve. Whenever possible, monkeys are housed together. They are stimulated with puzzles that earn them food rewards and toys. When animals have to be killed so their bodies can be studied, they are humanely euthanised.

"For now at least, as a society, we have decided that it is reasonable and ethical to do a certain amount of basic biomedical research using animal models," says Gordon. "But that's if, and only if, we do it in a very, very humane fashion."

What is your opinion?: How to write a persuasive argument

1. State your opinion

Think about the issues related to your topic. What is your opinion?

2. Research

Research the information you need to support your opinion.

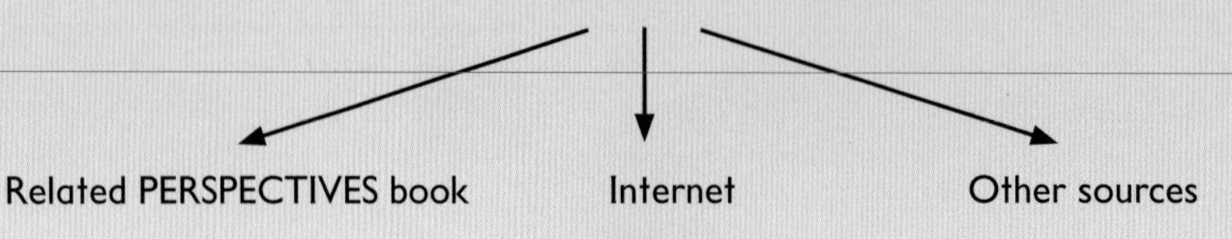

Related PERSPECTIVES book

Internet

Other sources

3. Make a plan

Introduction

How will you "hook" the reader?

State your opinion.

List reasons to support your opinion.

What persuasive devices will you use?

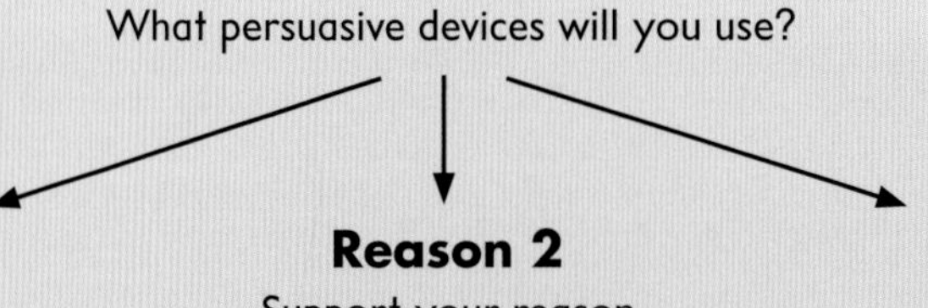

Reason 1
Support your reason
with evidence and details.

Reason 2
Support your reason
with evidence and details.

Reason 3
Support your reason
with evidence and details.

Conclusion

Restate your opinion. Leave your reader with a strong message.

4. Publish

Publish your persuasive argument.

Use visuals to reinforce your opinion.